GROSS BODY SCIENCE

RUMBLE & SPEW

GROSS STUFF IN YOUR STOMACH AND INTESTINES

Written by Sandy Donovan

Illustrated by Michael Slack

Millbrook Press • Minneapolis

For Henry, my favorite Rumbler,
and Gus, my favorite Spewer
—Sandy Donovan

To Ben Walker, the fastest guns
this side of Remington Ridge
-Michael Slack

Text copyright © 2010 by Sandy Donovan
Illustrations copyright © 2010 by Michael Slack

Millbrook Press
A division of Lerner Publishing Group, Inc.
241 First Avenue North
Minneapolis, MN 55401 U.S.A.

Website address: www.lernerbooks.com

Library of Congress Cataloging-in-Publication Data

Donovan, Sandra, 1967–
   Rumble & spew : gross stuff in your stomach and intestines / by Sandy Donovan ;
illustrated by Michael Slack.
     p.   cm. — (Gross body science)
   Includes bibliographical references and index.
   ISBN 978-0-8225-8899-3 (lib. bdg. : alk. paper)
   1. Gastrointestinal system—Juvenile literature. 2. Gastrointestinal system—
Diseases—Juvenile literature. I. Slack, Michael H., 1969– II. Title.
QP145.D68 2010
612.3—dc22   2008037713

Manufactured in the United States of America
1 2 3 4 5 6 — BP — 15 14 13 12 11 10

CONTENTS

ONE BIG ACID BATH

YOUR STOMACH

You've probably heard of acid. It's that stuff that can burn a hole right through your skin. It can even chew through metal. Yikes—better keep it away from your body, right?

So here's a question. What part of your body makes almost 4 pints (1.7 liters) of acid every day? It's your stomach! Your stomach is like a magician. It's job is to change the food you eat into a gloopy ball of gunk. That gunk-making process is called digestion. Your stomach needs acid to do this job well. To make sure it has enough acid, it makes its own. And then it squirts that acid all over itself.

Acid dissolves metal in this science experiment. Acid in your stomach works much the same way.

This hamburger is about to become gooey goop.

IT'S A SLIMY JOB

In a way, your stomach is like a reverse factory. Think about it. Factories take in raw materials like metal. Then they make complex items like cars. Your stomach takes in complex items. (What, you say? You don't think food is so complicated? Just picture all the different ingredients in a burger loaded with cheese, mustard, ketchup, pickles, and onions.) Then the stomach makes raw materials like vitamins and protein.

Well, your stomach doesn't do all of that by itself. It's just one step in the long digesting process. The whole slimy business begins even before you take a bite of food.

Digestion starts in your mouth when you think about taking a bite of food.

At the thought of food, your mouth begins to make saliva, or spit. Saliva helps soften food enough for you to swallow it. It's also essential for making spitballs. But you don't know anything about those, right?

When you chew your food, your teeth grind it into a saliva-soaked paste. **MMMM...DELICIOUS!** Then your tongue helps push the mushed-up food down your throat. After the throat, the food travels on through a tube called the esophagus. Right at the end of the esophagus is a muscle called the sphincter. This ring-shaped muscle lets food into the stomach. Once the food has passed through, the muscle squeezes shut to keep it from coming back the other way.

The sphincter muscle at the bottom of the esophagus helps keep food from coming back out of the stomach.

Here's what the sphincter looks like from inside the stomach.

INSIDE YOUR PERSONAL ACID FACTORY

On the outside, your stomach doesn't seem too gross. But on the inside, this little organ can get pretty nasty. Let's just say, it's probably best that you can't see—or feel—inside your stomach. Imagine sticking your hand into a bowl of slimy, cooked macaroni. Now imagine that the **macaroni is floating in a sauce of chewed-up food.** That's almost as gross as it would feel to stick your hand inside a stomach.

The stomach's inner walls are lined with thousands of rugae. No, rugae aren't a type of candy bar or a fancy new kind of gum. They're ripply flaps and folds on the inside of your stomach.

Rugae let the stomach stretch out when it's full of mashed-up food. Those rugae must be very busy after a big Thanksgiving dinner!

And it gets worse! The rugae are full of tiny holes. These little holes are like mini squirt guns. They shoot out stomach acid and other juices. The acidy juice surrounds food and breaks it down into a goopy mush.

So if this acid is so strong, how come it doesn't just burn a hole right through the walls of the stomach? Lucky for you, your stomach knows how to handle the acid. A thick layer of slimy mucus coats your stomach. The acid can't eat through the mucus, so the walls of your stomach are safe. What a relief!

Mucus (purple) hangs out in the stomach lining.

GROSS
FACT #1

Think of your stomach as a big, wrinkled balloon filled with mucus and acid. When it's empty, it's barely big enough to hold a mouthful of water. But it can stretch large enough to hold almost 1 gallon (3.8 liters) of food.

What happens to food in your stomach after the acid attack is done? It becomes a thick, gooey goop called chyme. But chyme can't be just any goop. It has to have a certain goopiness before it can leave your stomach. In fact, at the exit from the stomach, there's a **"GOOP TEST."** Well, it's not exactly a test—there's no pencil or paper and no teacher to grade it. But you have another sphincter connecting your stomach to your small intestines. Chyme has to be gooey enough to slide through this tube before it can leave the stomach. Once it can slide through the tube, it gets squirted into the small intestines.

An X-ray of the intestines reveals the twisty tubing that digests your food.

MUSHING AND MASHING

Have you ever wondered what food looks like inside your stomach? If you really want to find out, take a soaking wet kitchen towel and stuff some food inside it. Go ahead—stick something really goopy in there, like a part of a ham, tomato, and mayonnaise sandwich. Then roll the towel around the food and start wringing it out like you're trying to get all the water out of it. Make sure you twist it and turn it many different ways. Then—if you're brave—unwrap it and see what the contents look like. Now imagine squirting some real stomach acid into the mess. **CONGRATULATIONS!** You've made your own chyme. Um, who's going to clean that up?

Breaking down food isn't stomach acid's only job. It also attacks any bacteria that have gotten into the stomach. **WHAT? BACTERIA IN YOUR STOMACH?** *Someone call the doctor!* Wait, not so fast. In fact, your stomach's

WHAT'S THAT NOISE?

Ever heard of borborygmi? No, they're not some big, bad aliens from the latest sci-fi movie. They're those growling and rumbling sounds that your stomach makes. The sounds come from your stomach muscles grinding away as you're digesting your food. They happen most often about two to three hours after eating. Some people think the noises are a call for more food. But really, they're just the happy sounds of digestion.

GROWL

RUMBLE

BORBORYGMI

full of these tiny
living things.
Some are good
for you, but
many are bad.
Stomach acid attacks and kills
the bad ones before they can make you ill.
So are you feeling sick? No? Well, where are your
manners? You'd better say, "thank you" to that helpful
stomach acid!

WHEN ACID ACTS UP

Ugh—what could be grosser than the sloppy business
that goes on inside your stomach? **Just be glad your
skin isn't see-through—then you'd never be
able to forget that churning mess
going on inside your belly.** Except
for the occasional gurgle and growl,
you could go through your day
unaware of the goop inside
your stomach.

13

The average kid digests almost 1,000 pounds (450 kilograms) of food each year. In your lifetime, that could add up to more than 50 tons (45 metric tons). That weighs as much as seven full-grown elephants!

1000

OWWWW!

But don't get too comfy. Every once in a while, stomach acid reminds people that it's around. One of the ways it does this is to sneak back up into the esophagus. Remember the sphincter that food passes through to get to the stomach? It's only supposed to let things through one way—from esophagus to stomach. But every once in a while, it lets something slip through the wrong way. Then some stomach acid ends up in the esophagus. And you can probably guess that stomach acid doesn't feel—or taste—very good.

When acid hits the walls of your esophagus, you'll know it. Have you ever felt a burning, itching feeling at the bottom of your throat? That's stomach acid. **That feeling is often called heartburn.** It feels like burning because that's what acid does—it burns. Don't worry—it doesn't actually get to your heart. But that doesn't make it any more fun.

Acid can also burn right into your stomach. Remember that thick coat of mucus that protects the stomach walls from the acid? Well sometimes that layer gets too thin and the acid starts to get through. (Why does the mucus layer get too thin? *Heliobacter pylori* bacteria can cause this.) Then the acid attacks the stomach walls. Soon there's an open, festering sore called an ulcer where the acid is eating away at the stomach's lining. Ugg—just thinking about that is enough to make you feel downright queasy.

A stomach ulcer

CHAPTER 2

WHAT GOES IN MUST COME OUT

ALL ABOUT POOP

Still not grossed out? Well, hold on tight. Because if picturing a churning stomach full of acid-coated goop didn't do it, then this next section just might send you running.

The chyme that leaves your stomach gets turned into the most repulsive goop of all. Yep, it's time to make poop. You might call it feces, fecal matter, waste, number two, or poop. Or you might prefer to call it nothing at all.

Here's a microscopic view of your small intestines—another stop your food makes on its way to becoming poop!

Poop is nasty stuff. It's basically a lump of all the leftovers your body wants to get rid of. Here's a quick look at how our bodies make it—and how they get rid of it.

POOP FACTORY

Your stomach may be like a reverse factory, but your intestines are just a plain old poop-making machine. **Remember the goopy chyme that gets squirted into the small intestine? That's poop's star ingredient.** Chyme has the look and feel—but definitely not the taste!— of melted ice cream. But don't get grossed out yet—it gets worse. Before it gets turned into poop, it passes through both of your intestines and has a couple more gross things added in.

Did you know you're walking around with a slimy 20-foot (6-meter) tube coiled up inside you? Your small intestine is only about 1 inch (2.5 centimeters) wide. But if it were stretched out end to end, it would be almost five times as tall as you!

FIRST STOP: small intestine. This long, rubbery tube makes sure that every bit of nutrition is squeezed out of the goop before it becomes poop. To help with this job, the small intestine has thousands of fingerlike projections called villi. They poke and prod the chyme as it travels through the intestines. They are literally stirring up the goop. They also take in nutrients and send them out to the rest of the body.

NEXT STOP: large intestine. There, the melted-ice-cream-like goop becomes full-fledged poop. The first order of business is

A close-up of small intestine villi

This goblet cell releases a glob of mucus in the intestines.

getting rid of some of the extra water in the chyme. The walls of the intestines absorb the water. And while they're at it, the large intestine throws in a few more waste products. First, any old dead, used-up cells that are floating around get mixed in. Next come any extra bacteria that have been hanging around. Now the goop is less goopy and more like a mushy piece of, well, poop.

TIME TO EXIT

Poop has one more stop—the rectum—before its ready to go. The rectum is actually the last third of the large intestine. It's where poop hangs out until you deposit it into the toilet. (Or into a bush on the side of the road if you just can't wait any longer!)

GROSS FACT #4

Your large intestine needs help moving poop along. So to keep things moving, the intestine coats itself in slimy mucus. The mucus allows the poop to glide right on through. Happy trails!

When enough poop collects in the rectum, you'll feel that familiar urge. If everything's working well, you'll find a toilet. Then you'll use your rectum muscles to push the poop right on out. It exits through an opening called the anus. Most people poop one or two times a day. Some people poop at exactly the same time every day. They can almost set their watches by their regular toilet time! Others aren't so lucky. They can feel that urge almost any time of the day.

Wonder how much poop you really poop? Most people poop about 1 ounce (28 grams) of poop for each 12 pounds (5.4 kg) they weigh.

This close-up shows several kinds of bacteria present in poop.

NEED A WIPE?

Have you ever found yourself stranded after pooping with no toilet paper in sight? All your options are pretty gross, right? But did you know that people haven't always used toilet paper?

SO WHAT DID PEOPLE DO WITHOUT TP? They found all sorts of ways to clean up after pooping. Lots of people used leaves or rocks. Some people in cold climates used snow. Some people who lived near the ocean used shells. On the Hawaiian Islands, coconut shells were the tool of choice. The ancient Romans wrapped a wet rag around a stick. After wiping, they rinsed the rag in a bucket of salt water.

After the printing press was invented in the mid-1400s, lots of people could get their hands on paper. Old newspapers were very handy for wiping. And after Europeans came to the Americas, they found a brand-new tool. Well, first, they found a brand-new crop—corn. And then they learned a great use for used corncobs.

Finally, in 1857, the first pack of toilet paper was sold. But it was expensive and didn't really catch on. About thirty-five years later, a company rolled the paper around a tube. Toilet paper as we know it was born.

So if you weigh 100 pounds (45 kg), you're probably dumping about half a pound (0.2 kilogram) of poop in the toilet each time you go. Sometimes it's less, and sometimes it's more. And sometimes, it's so much more that it's a *TWO-FLUSHER!*

Did you know poop can talk?

Well, not really, but it can tell you a lot about yourself. Mostly it reflects what you eat. If you eat a lot of meat, your pieces of poop will probably be small and dark. If you eat lots of fresh vegetables, you'll have more poop.

I KNOW WHAT YOU'VE BEEN EATING.

If you want to really examine your poop (do you really want to?), you'll see even more evidence of what you've eaten. Some things—like corn—look almost the same after they come out as they did when they went in. Other things leave behind traces of color. Got yellow poop? You've probably been drinking lots of milk. And if you eat beets, you may notice a reddish color to your turds.

Did you know that if you eat corn, you can often see whole kernels in your poop?

GROSS FACT #5

Want to see blue green poop? I can't imagine why you would, but you can try eating a lot of blueberries. That just might do the trick.

23

CHAPTER 3

GAS ATTACK

BELCHES AND FARTS

You know the feeling. You're enjoying your lunch at school. You take a bite of sandwich and swallow. Then you take a sip of your drink. Suddenly, before you can stop it, out rings a loud **BUUURRP.** If your friends are like a lot of kids, they probably start laughing. Then someone else rips a ringing belch. Before you know it, you're in the middle of a full-fledged burping contest. Uh—until a teacher shows up, that is.

But what if the scene is different? What if, instead of eating lunch with your friends, you're sitting in the classroom? What would you do if you suddenly felt a burp then? Would you be able to stop it in time?

Sometimes there's just no stopping a burp.

JUST WHAT IS A BURP?

Some kids are extra talented at making themselves burp. But most of the time, burping is just a natural bodily function. Once your body begins to burp, there's often nothing you can do to stop it. Sometimes, you just have to let it rip.

A burp is simply gas escaping from your stomach. Gas in your stomach? Yep, you might be surprised to know how much gas really is in your stomach. Most of it gets there from the air you swallow. Air is full of gases, especially nitrogen, oxygen, and carbon dioxide.

Think you don't swallow much air? Think again. Every time you take a bite of food or a sip of a drink, you swallow a little air. And if you happen to gulp your food or drink, well, then you swallow a lot of air. The more air you swallow, the more gas you trap in your stomach. (Hmm, are you getting an idea of how you could really improve your belching skills?)

But swallowing air isn't the only way to trap gas in your stomach. Think about it. **What's something that really makes you belch? Soda! A can of soda is full of carbon dioxide.** So every time you guzzle a soda, you end up with a bellyful of gas. Doesn't that feel nice?

BRA-A-A-A-AP!

BELCH SODA with CARBON DIOXIDE

Your stomach can find uses for just about any kind of food you swallow. But it really wants nothing to do with gas. All gas does is make it bloat and feel like a balloon. So what happens when you've got a bellyful of unwanted gas? Back up it comes. Remember that sphincter muscle between the stomach and the esophagus? Its job is to let food and drink pass through only one way—in the direction of the stomach. But when it feels a burp coming, it opens up in a hurry. Up shoots the gas. And before you know it, out comes a belch. It's up to you whether to be proud or embarrassed.

GROSS FACT #6

The more air you swallow, the bigger your burp. So if you want to really impress friends and family, take a few big gulps of air and belch away.

American Idol winner Kelly Clarkson lets one rip during a burping contest.

WHAT'S THAT SMELL?

Quick Question: You accidentally let out a LOUD, STINKY fart. What do you do?

a.) Look around and smile proudly.

b.) Act innocent and go about your business.

c.) Blame the dog or the person standing next to you.

Your answer probably depends on the situation. If you're hanging out with your friends, you may want to take credit for your masterpiece. The louder the fart, the more impressed they'll be. But if you're in class, you may want to play innocent. And if you're at your grandmother's house, you might be tempted to blame her dog. (You may already know, however, that this excuse hardly ever fools anybody!)

Everybody breaks wind. (That's another way to say fart. A more scientific way to say it is flatulence.) Movie stars do it. World-class athletes do it. Even the president does it! Polite people try not to fart in public, but sometimes they just can't help themselves. Like belches, farts occur when trapped gases escape from the digestive system. But unlike belches, farts do not escape through the mouth. **(THANK GOODNESS, THEY'D TASTE TERRIBLE!)**

RESEARCH PROJECT

On averae, healthy people fart about fourteen times per day. To see how you measure up, take some notes. Make yourself a fart diary, and start tracking your farts each day. If you want to get even more detailed, you can also write down all the food you eat. Then rate your farts for loudness and stink factor. See any patterns between the food you eat and the farts you make?

A belch is gas escaping from the stomach. If gas makes it to the intestines, it comes out as a fart instead of a burp. Most farts are caused by swallowed air. By the time this air reaches the intestines, it contains mostly carbon dioxide and nitrogen. These two gases cause bubbles, but they don't have much of an odor. When they escape as farts, they are often loud but not so stinky. Some people call these thunder bombs.

But we all know there's another kind of toot: the silent but deadly (SBD) fart. What makes these different from thunder bombs? These quiet stink bombs are not caused by swallowed air. Instead, they're made when undigested food gets into the intestines. The intestines are full of healthful bacteria. These bugs attack whatever food enters their home. Sounds gross, but they are really helping us out. They finish breaking down any remaining food into nutrients.

GROSS FACT #7

The ancient Romans believed that holding in farts could damage a person's health. The emperor Claudius passed a law making it legal to fart at the table!

They work to break down food. And give you stinky gas in the process.

But there's one small side effect. While the bacteria are attacking the food, they create new gases. These particular gases are *stinky*. And what do gases do when they get trapped in the intestines? They find a quick way to exit! But these gases are not full of bubbles. So they don't escape with an explosion. Instead, they creep out, silent but deadly!

THUNDER BOMB

SBD

HEAT BLAST

Are some farts warmer than others? Yes! Thunder bombs exit your body at about body temperature. But SBDs can feel quite warm as they escape. That's because the digestion process that makes them also creates heat. And some of this heat gets carried right on out as you fart.

Did YOU just fart?

Of course, not all farts are equal. What you eat has a lot to do with the farts you make. Even those loud, not-so-stinky farts can pick up some odors on their way through your intestines. Certain vegetables such as cauliflower and cabbage produce particularly foul-smelling toots. Other stink producers are eggs, meat, and milk. **If you want to achieve a truly thunderous fart, eat lots of beans.** Mix and match your foods, and you can brew some superfarts that are both loud *and* stinky!

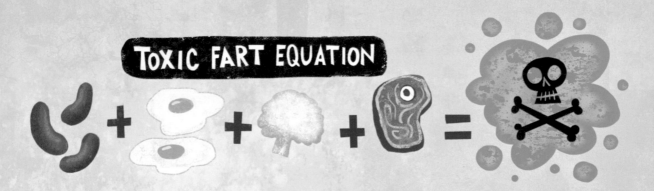

TOXIC FART EQUATION

CHAPTER 4

RUMBLING and SPEWING

WHEN YOU GET SICK

Even when everything's humming along smoothly, your digestive system can create some pretty rancid products. Belches, farts, and poop are all perfectly natural—and healthy—events. So what happens when things aren't going so smoothly? As you can imagine, the results can be pretty revolting. Rumbling in the stomach can cause spewing from two places.

SOMETIMES WHAT GOES DOWN MUST COME UP

Vomit. Barf. Spew. Ralph. Puke. Throw up. Hurl. Blow chunks. There are plenty of words for what happens when your stomach sends food back up and out of your mouth. But whatever you call it, the end result probably looks as bad as it tastes.

Puking is one way your body protects itself from disease. Two things can make your stomach sick enough to vomit. One is a virus. A virus is a tiny organism that gets into your cells and multiplies, making you sick in the process. Your body vomits to get rid of the virus. The other common cause of vomiting is food poisoning. **This occurs when you eat bad food.**

FOOD POISON *Buffet*

(And no, we're not talking about chopped liver or bean curd—we mean spoiled or rotten food.) Almost all the food we eat has some bacteria in it. Most bacteria are harmless. But some bacteria are bad news. Usually your stomach and intestines can handle these harmful bugs before they bother you.

E. coli

A SHORT LIST OF FOODS THAT CAN MAKE YOU BARF

- Beef, chicken, or fish that has been contaminated with either *E. coli* bacteria or *Salmonella* bacteria
- Eggs or milk that has spoiled (that's why they print those dates on the packages)
- Any food with meat or dairy in it that has been left at room temperature for more than a couple of hours. This lets bacteria grow all over it!

Once in a while, your body takes in more bad bacteria than you can deal with. That's when your stomach throws itself into reverse. It's time to clear things out, and you know what that means. It's hurling time.

When you have a virus or eat bad food, you may feel a stomachache for a few hours. But when it's time to vomit, you'll have to act fast. Once your stomach sends that message, you won't have much time to find the bathroom. Your stomach muscles contract. They're pushing the food back out. Then the sphincter muscle at the top of the stomach opens to let the mess up into

GROSS FACT #8

People who puke too often can get rotten teeth from all that stomach acid meeting up with their tooth enamel—eeewww!

your esophagus. If lots of stomach acid has already been mixed in with the chewed-up food, you may notice a burning feeling in your throat. And then, well, let's just hope you made it to the bathroom—or at least found a bucket—in time.

Vomit comes in all sorts of shapes and colors. Do you have a favorite color for your vomit? Sometimes it has bits of undigested food in it. If you've just eaten vegetables, you'll probably see chunks of veggies in the vomit. If you've eaten something with a strong color or smell, you may notice that too. **YUCK!**

If you vomit food that's already made it out of your stomach and into your intestines, it may be coated in an extra-gross green slime. That slime is called bile. It's a juice that helps you digest fats. Bile is made in the liver and meets up with food in your small intestine. And it makes vomit look even nastier than plain old stomach vomit.

Just about the only good thing about vomiting is that you usually feel a little better right after you spew. If your stomach has been really upset and then you vomit, your stomach will be happy that it's gotten rid of whatever was bothering it. But beware! You may get that yucky feeling again pretty soon. Most people vomit more than once when they have a stomach virus or food poisoning. Sometimes your body keeps trying to make you vomit even after your stomach is empty. This is often called the dry heaves—and believe me, it's nothing you want to suffer through.

Thar he blows!

Rotavirus (the round spheres) is a leading cause of diarrhea.

UH-OH, GOTTA RUN

A virus or food poisoning can give you problems on the other end as well. Sometimes an upset stomach will warn you that something's not right. Other times, you'll suddenly realize that you've got to make it to the bathroom—**FAST!** (And you may have to stay there for a while too.)

GROSS FACT #9

On average, people get diarrhea about four times a year. Each time, the body dumps about 1 quart (1 liter) of runny poop per day.

Diarrhea, also known as the runs, or the squirts, is when you have watery, runny poop. In fact, your poop has gotten so liquidy that you can't keep it in. Diarrhea usually starts because you've eaten something bad. Or you may have an infection in your large intestine. The food's already traveled too far from the stomach to be returned as vomit. So, out the other end it flows.

GROSS FACT 10

If you're really unlucky, you might be vomiting and getting diarrhea at the same time. When you've got it "coming out of both ends," you know you're in tough shape. That's when you need a toilet and a bucket at the same time!

Remember those healthful bacteria that live in your intestines? They're the ones that attack undigested food and cause those SBD farts. Those same bacteria also attack any sickness-causing bugs that make it into your intestines. And then, stand aside—**it's the battle of the bugs.** Usually the good bugs win, and you never feel a thing. But when the bad bugs win, well, you'd better find a bathroom, **PRONTO!**

ALL STOPPED UP?

Having the runs is no fun, but neither is the opposite. When you just can't poop, you're constipated. You may feel full and bloated. You may feel like you need to poop, but you just can't do it. This sometimes happens when you don't eat enough fiber—a substance found in fruits, vegetables, and whole grains. So it seems like eating extra fiber would help solve the problem, right? Wrong! Once you're constipated, extra fiber will just back up your jammed intestines. Instead, try fruit juices like prune or apple or ask your parents about medicine.

Diarrhea is sloppy, stinky, and not much fun at all. But remember, it's just your body getting rid of unhealthy invaders. Your body often needs more than one release of watery poop to get your digestive system back on track. That's why, when you have the runs, you'll want to stick pretty close to a toilet. Otherwise, you could find yourself needing to sprint to make it there on time. And despite the name, the runs don't help you run any faster.

BACK TO NORMAL

Barfing and having the runs can really ruin your day. But as bad as they may seem at the time, they're important parts of helping your body get back to normal. Your body needs to get rid of unwanted visitors. And the sooner it can do this, the better. Once they're gone, your body can get back to the business of making acid, turning food into mush, belching, pooping, and farting!

GLOSSARY

bacteria: microscopic living things that exist all around and inside you

bile: a green liquid made by the liver that helps digest food

borborygmi: the growling and rumbling sounds the digestive system makes as it breaks down food

chyme: mashed-up food that has already been digested by the stomach

esophagus: a tube that carries food from the throat to the stomach

feces: solid waste that leaves your body

organ: a part of the body such as the stomach or the heart that does a particular job

protein: a nutrient made up of building blocks called amino acids. Protein helps build bones and muscles.

rectum: the last part of the large intestines, which ends at the opening called the anus

rugae: ripply folds on the inside wall of the stomach

sphincter: a ring of muscles that open and close to allow substances, such as food, to pass through. The stomach's entrance and exit are both sphincters

villi: small, fingerlike projections in the intestines that pull nutrients out of the food you eat

virus: a microscopic living organism that causes disease

vitamin: a nutrient needed by the body for normal functioning and good health

SELECTED BIBLIOGRAPHY

Bowen, Richard. "Pathology of the Digestive System." *Colorado State University*. July 5, 2006. http://www.vivo.colostate.edu/hbooks/pathphys/digestion/index.html (December 18, 2008).

Gray, Henry. *Anatomy of the Human Body*. Philadelphia: Lea & Febiger, 1990.

Marieb, Elaine N. *Anatomy & Physiology*. San Francisco: Benjamin Cummings, 2002.

National Institutes of Health. "Your Digestive System and How It Works." *National Digestive Diseases Information Clearinghouse (NDDIC)*. April 2008. http://digestive.niddk.nih.gov/ddiseases/pubs/yrdd/index.htm (December 18, 2008).

SIGBio. "The Digestive System." *Virtual Anatomy Textbook*. N.d. http://www.acm.uiuc.edu/sigbio/project/digestive/ (December 18, 2008).

FURTHER READING

Ballard, Carol. *The Stomach and Digestion*. New York: Franklin Watts, 2005. Read more details about how your body digests food.

The Digestive System
  http://www.innerbody.com/image/digeov.html
  View detailed pictures of the human digestive system—and find definitions for all the parts—at this interactive site.

Human Digestive System
  http://www.enchantedlearning.com/subjects/anatomy/digestive/
  Discover more interesting facts about digestion. You can also print a diagram of the human digestive system.

KidsHealth
  http://www.kidshealth.org/kid/
  Learn more about the digestive system at this information-packed website, made especially for kids. Check out the Game Closet to view videos about the digestive system and other bodily functions.

Parker, Steve. *Break It Down: The Digestive System*. Chicago: Raintree, 2006. This informative book includes full-color diagrams of the digestive system.

Singer, Marilyn. *What Stinks?* Plain City, OH: Darby
Creek Publishing, 2006. Find out about all kinds
of foul odors—whether from humans, animals, or
plants—in this look about bad smells.

INDEX

About the Author

Sandy Donovan has written many books for young readers. She lives in Minneapolis and is an expert on farting and belching thanks to her sons, Henry and Gus.

About the Illustrator

Michael Slack's illustrations have appeared in books, magazines, advertisements, and on TV. His paintings and drawings have been exhibited in the United States and Europe. Michael lives in the San Francisco Bay area.

Photo Acknowledgments